Tooth Box

Jenny Irish

Spuyten Duyvil
New York City

© 2022 Jenny Irish
ISBN 978-1-956005-32-5

cover art: Katy Horan

Library of Congress Cataloging-in-Publication Data

Names: Irish, Jenny (Jenny H.), author.
Title: Tooth box / Jenny Irish.
Description: New York City : Spuyten Duyvil, [2022] |
Identifiers: LCCN 2021048611 | ISBN 9781956005325 (paperback)
Subjects: LCGFT: Poetry.
Classification: LCC PS3609.R56 T66 2022 | DDC 811/.6--dc23
LC record available at https://lccn.loc.gov/2021048611

For Celia

Contents

Girlhood	7
The Woman Who had the Job	9
Seriously	11
Due	15
The *Motherfucker*	17
Heirlooms	19
Ribbon	22
Patsy Cline	23
Deadeye	25
Fire Season	26
Hungers	27
Mothers	29
Viola	31
Tides	34
Possibilities	36
Birdsong	38
Balance	40
Tooth Box	41
Was	44
The Right Word	45
Kindness	46
Bites	48
Wolves	49
Fiddlehead	53
Pearls	55
Wonders	57
O	60
Spirals	62
Denouement	65
Attic	70
In Texas There Are Tours of Things That Aren't There Anymore	73

Girlhood

Fifteen years ago, I was any girl in girlhood.

All the parts were there: the summer and the softness of the sand, the greenish pond ringed by rocks and pines, the catcalls, and the birdsong too, and the strokes of skin bare to the hot eye of the sun, and the hidden skin too, where nothing, not even daylight, touched, and around my shoulders a smell, rinsed, but not quite clean.

The days passed like water between cupped hands.

Mornings, seven-days-a-week, I wore a white scalloped apron, poured coffee for tourists and college students rowdy on summer break, and in the afternoons was released into salted heat, seagulls swooping overhead, and my best friend waiting, barefoot on her brother's borrowed bike, twisting the end of her ponytail, skinny, bikinied, and perpetually bored.

She handled me like a boy would his freshest little love, balancing the bike so I could mount behind her. We rode, her hair blowing back into my mouth and eyes.

The nights were long and were my own.

I had a mother who was somewhere else pretending she was someone else.

I took long baths, read longer books, fell asleep hot with the lights on, and woke to five a.m. sunrise and the clattering of adolescent crows.

I could not anticipate envy—that at thirty. I would covet the shapely limbs of the girls who pour my morning coffee into its paper cup, every move a new peek of pretty skin, their tops cut low to show their lace bras and sweet freckled backs.

Once, I was near naked on the rocks and my eyes were closed against the shine of water, closed against tomorrow and another day when I would serve coffee and then oil myself sleek as a seal, spreading the water in front of me until I was bored with the easy work of opening the thousand little eyelet hooks of its cool clasp, closed against another day when the only word that fit me was *young*.

The Woman Who had the Job

The woman who had the job before I had the job was supposed to train me for a month. That was the plan. I would start in July and she would leave in August and we would, like waves, or words, or worries, overlap. But my contract was caught-up in an airconditioned current drifting back and forth between the breezy offices of upper administrators who had more pressing business, or were in Europe for the summer.

I could not officially start, but the woman who had the job before I had the job was overwhelmed, and overworked, and overtired, and over *it*, by which I mean the work, which was, in my mind, important work, and work that had to be done, and we had, she and I, developed a quirky little friendship that did not require us to speak, so I sat by her extra shoes—heels for meetings, flats for comfort—and sorted shiny sheaves of violet-gray mimeographs destined for the shredder while she toggled back and forth between two computer screens: one vital records, the other classifieds for sunny studio apartments in another state. Knowing she would leave let her stay a little longer.

The woman who had the job before I had the job had a young, freckled face on a fragile body that made me think of little girls at swimming lessons, in Maine, in February, when the snow covered the skylights above the pool and made the air violet-gray, with a softness like the fur of an animal that is gray, but whose coat is called blue. She provoked an off-kilter synesthesia, a hallucinatory chill up my spine like the vibrations of bright, percussive metal. She made me think of little girls who shivered before they were wet.

I liked the woman who had the job before I had the job very much, though she made me homesick for a place I had not lived for a dozen years. Sometimes, like a child, she would forget that I was there, sitting quiet among her shoes, and she would sing herself a made-up song: *Leaving, leaving, I'm leaving for good.*

The woman who had the job before I had the job left, and I took her place. Men who had accused her of incompetence accused me of incompetence, told me their dreams about dolphins, forgot what they had said, returned and said it all again, and asked the single same suspicious question: *Why do you look different?*

Seriously

Thanks are owed to the longhaired rabbit who would sigh and stretch, turning into my hands while I used an antique hairpin to pick loose the knots along her belly.

She would put her teeth on me, a gentle warning without warning, raising a red thread of blood.

She would hold my finger in her mouth, helping me to understand that she could cut me to the bone and through it: abbreviate the hand that touched her, amputate the touch, if the touch was wrong.

*

I dug a grave and faced it with sharp shards of shale because the stone was her long coat's color and to have a reason to say *cairn*.

*

My father did not burn me on purpose, but was careless with his cigarettes, a bored, impatient smoker, a bored, impatient boy.

*

I was a quiet girl, curious with my body, learning *hot* by touch.

*

Driving with the windows down, my father flicked hot ash, and it blew back into my face, red for the moment of its quick bite then white and soft like the perfumed powder my mother's mother patted along her long white thighs.

*

There is a difference, my father's stepmother said, between being shameless and being unwilling to be ashamed.

*

As a child, I squat in the pinewoods, chewed wintergreen and drank from a still-water pond divoted with mosquitoes, shallow water full with weather-shattered plastic shotguns shells. I knew better than to drink from it and drank, but was never made sick, until I saw, swallowing from cupped hands, a carcassed deer, half submerged, the remains of butchering pushing from black plastic, and the head was loose: the purple thrust of the muscle of the tongue, the visible eye whited-out by maggots.

*

The teenage boys who lived through the woods hid their magazines in a fort made from scavenged boards and tin roofing: centerfolds of shiny red cars and centerfolds of spread vaginas held open by fingernails painted shiny red.

*

When I was a little girl, a teenage girl was grabbed from the side of a country road and forced into the far back of a wood-paneled station wagon, where another girl was stuffed into a brown paper grocer's bag, only her little legs in white knit tights with pink knit hearts showing.

*

The blackberry canes were flowering, ice-white for the start of Spring. Men beat the brambles down, stabbed sticks down into the shin-deep murky meltwater of roadside ditches. They called: *Little girl, little girl—*

Men, who I imagine must have haunted themselves down into exhaustion, if not true sleep, to then dress again in the dark before morning, hunting their yards for a deadfall stick to use for feeling the underbrush for a body.

A white thread was found woven through an abandoned bird's nest.

*

What girl on a bicycle, braids blowing behind her, hasn't been followed by a man in a truck mounted with a spotlight for freezing deer dead-still in the fields at night, the brightness turning their eyes lavender-white, and what girl hasn't also known a girl who hasn't invented for herself a violation, hasn't squirmed into a victim's borrowed skin like secret-slipping into her sister's dress to shimmy at the mirror, basking in the play-pretend of being called beautiful, of being called brave?

*

When I was a little girl, a teenage girl lied and said she was grabbed from the side of a country road and forced into the far back of a wood-paneled station wagon, where another girl was stuffed into a brown paper grocer's bag, only her little legs in white knit tights with pink knit hearts showing.

*

By the blue television light of the nightly news, the babysitter's boyfriend brushed out and braided my hair. He said: *What girls do now is just say somebody fiddled 'em, and they get away with murder.*

*

When I was a girl, I worked with a man whose favorite joke was wordplay: katydids and a girl from the distant days of his youth who all the boys at his school had called Katie-Did.

*

An investigator working on behalf of my employer contacted me. The subject of the call was a claim of sexual harassment reported by a third party and denied by the alleged victim. When I said I had never seen nor sensed any indication of impropriety, the investigator asked again if I had ever seen or sensed any indication of impropriety, and when I said again that I had never seen nor sensed any indication of impropriety, the investigator asked if it were possible that I did not have the experience to understand the complexities of gender-based power dynamics. She said: *We take such matters seriously.*

Due

For much of my young life, I lived
in the daily violence of an unhappy home—
a pretty young mother sick with regret
for the children that bound her to a fat
and miserable boy, whose belligerent
football bulk began to hurt his knees
before he was even twenty, and who knew
that his wife and his children could not stand him,
and would not, despite his most heartfelt efforts,
be battered into believing he was a man
who was good or deserving of respect.
But outside our unhappy home, I lived
the cosseted, cotton-batting-wrapped existence
of a hemophiliac infanta, my tender girlhood guarded
against all injury. Not until college, did I carry
a bag of groceries for myself, or step from a car
to pump my own gas. At the station, an attendant
in canvas coveralls wiped the crust of mayflies
from the headlights with a rag, and then, unasked,
brought me a can of pineapple soda, dripping with cold
from the ice-filled cooler inside, and at the sundae shoppe,
the old owner gave every girl an extra scoop of his hand-turned,
antique-colored French Vanilla to feed her sweetness.
Walking between the tents at the farmers' market,
I was invited to take a strawberry from the pints,
and the rancher selling paper wrapped cuts of meat
allowed me to pet the harnessed ewe in front of his stall,
to fondle the soft cones of her ears and talk about sweaters,
and never once told me that all lambs were not kept for
their fleece. But I knew, the way a duckling topples
into water and can swim, that this public performance
of men was balanced behind closed doors.
At the school carnival, I watched my father, with his bad knees,

lift girls one-after-another onto his wide shoulders
and gallop them around the playing field, whinnying like a horse,
his hands clubbed into hooves instead of fists.
I watched the girls put their hands in my father's hair,
pulling, giving commands—*Faster, horsey, faster*—
and I knew I was responsible to pay
what their fun and games made due.

The Motherfucker

It isn't really etched in stone, on a tablet, or on a great barnacled boulder, the chisel marks just edging from the ebbing sea as the tides pull out, or hidden, deep inside the darkness of a desert cave, waiting for the touch of torchlight, warm like the sun, that a woman must love the man she marries.

At the corner of my childhood's eye, at the periphery of the vision of memory, is a small man in a white coat with combed gray hair, tidy as a cat. My mother is mad for him, this man, sick with love, but I do not always know it. First, I am a little mistake of a child, quiet and hardly aware, and I do not even exist—I am actual nothing—when the small, tidy man first approaches my mother, knowing nothing about her except that she is young and pretty, and that, really, really that is all he wants to know: she is young, and she is pretty. These are the qualities that interest him.

These qualities interest the small, tidy man enough that he can ignore the cheap gold band on her finger and the tiny boy she brings with her and tucks away in a nest of blankets when she works the overnight shift. The small, tidy man cannot imagine, I imagine, when he makes his first approach, the silver scars on my mother's concave stomach that he will later stroke, wanting for himself to be stroked in return.

Years later, my mother is still mad for the man, sick with love for his white coat, his combed gray hair, how he smells, always, slightly cold, from, she thinks, the industrial disinfectant and the powder inside the latex gloves on-and-off his small, smart hands all-day-long, all-night-long. I come across her, lying in her bed, with his stethoscope to her chest, whispering his name to hear her heart go faster, faster.

My brother calls the man The *Mother*fucker.

My mother is still mad for him, the small, tidy man with his white coat, and combed gray hair, and slight, cold smell, sick with love. When I make the trip from Boston to Portland on a Concord Trailways bus, so that I may officially meet him, despite having known the small, tidy man since I have had memory, my mother begs me to deliver a little line over dinner—my first with her and him, my mother and the small, tidy man, as an official item, though he still lives with a wife—insistent it will be funny. *A joke*, she says. *A joke*.

We are at a seafood shack eating fried platters, and though all I had wanted was a shrimp basket—shrimp fried in cornmeal with cocktail sauce—the small, tidy man has gotten us all platters, all three beer-battered and salted. He leaves the table and returns with tiny paper cups of tartar sauce, then leaves and returns with lemon wedges, then leaves, and my mother says, *A joke? A joke?* and then he is back again with two fistfuls of napkins.

Should I leave, should I leave and never be seen again, I believe the small, tidy man will easily forget that I ever was. What girl, vanished? What girl, gone in the night? So, what does it matter, what I say, when it is impossible that I will make any kind of impression? Already, for years, I have made none. So, I will deliver my mother's silly line, give her that, if that is what she really wants. So, to the small, tidy man, I say what my mother has asked me to say. The joke: *Does this mean you're my daddy?* Which, of course, we all already know, he is.

Heirlooms

Recurring—
the nightmare where I am eaten
with the tiny silver trident forks
for loosening the flesh from shelled bodies.

In it, I am laid out on a table laid
for lobster dinner with enough
chairs drawn all around
for all of my mother's family.

All women, and all strong,
if strength can be measure by standing
at a mirror, penciling clean black around eyes
you would as soon gouge out.

In this nightmare,
as in life.
my father and his family
do not exist. This, for some,
is a fantasy: a world of only women.

I am laid with my head still uncracked
in line-of-sight of the salt bowl.
where the cast-off milk-teeth
of puppies, now dogs, are mixed with
coarse flakes and herbs.

A finishing salt, to salt the wounds,
to flavor my bland body
being disassembled to enjoy.
Salt, they say, to taste.

Little hostess, little performer, little imitation
of a little girl imitating a mother,
I have served child-size, china-headed dolls
tea with the delicate bits of silverware
working me apart from inside of me.

Heirlooms, they were forbidden
as play things, but what forbidden things
have my fingers not touched and turned,
left ghosted with the grease of my graceless hands—

Family-passed-down-things,
called hers, or hers, or yours,
until she, or she, or you gifted them to me,
to be mine in the future, promised
upon a passing, I have already handled
in hiding, as if they were already mine.

All sleep, I know, is haunted,
the day that proceeded slinking
weasel-like, through the pinkish
give of the brain, leaving an oily
secretion to mark its territory.

Or, imagine instead,
the ghosts of experience
working in the gray mâché of the wrinkles
of the mind as wasps, industrious
in the walls of an already inhabited home,
building until ownership is theirs.

In sleep we cannot die,
but I have seen a living thing lured
into the baited confine of an ethical trap
that drops a gate and holds the nuisance captive
for release far away, where it will,
in theory, be no bother, but,
the drive, the drive to far away,
is, in-of-itself, a bother—

So, I have seen a hand make choices,
compress the thin metal skin
of a black bottle of pungent fluid for refilling
an initial-etched silver lighter, and I have
seen a magic matchhead—*Strike Anywhere*—
taken from an enameled box
on the mantle of a house
that only death may make mine,
cracked into ready flame.

Ribbon

If it is helpful, we can think of words
falling into one of three categories:
the spoken, the unspoken, and the unspeakable—

There are things that I want to say that I know
that I cannot say, that I know will be met by silence
and that will ensure that I am exiled from the eroding
island that is my family, worn smaller every year

My brother, for a time, worked in coastal protection,
part of a team tasked with designing underwater walls
that would alter the way the ocean ate at the shoreline,
but then his team's duty was changed to coastal restoration,
and they became responsible for designing underwater walls
that would protect millions of pounds of sand bought and brought
by a convoy of dump trucks from a quarry, added annually to the beaches

When I think of the things I want to say, in my mind,
I see myself standing in the kitchen with my tongue out,
the wet muscle pinched still between my thumb and index finger,
a wood handled paring knife in my other hand, ready to saw

Once, I was a member of the audience for a production of *Titus Andronicus*,
where for Lavinia—whose tongue is cut out and whose hands are cut off
to keep her from naming the men who first rape and then mutilate her
deep in the darkness of the woods to conceal their crimes—
there was a clever visual trick. Red ribbon streamers tied
at the actress's wrists: Lavinia trailing blood behind her
as long as a wedding train, and each time she opened her emptied mouth,
each time she tried to speak, but could not speak, a damp fist of red,
the ribbon packed tight against the actress's intact tongue, tumbled loose,
and so long before Lavinia's father—the Titus of the title—called her close,
held her to his chest, and chose to cut her throat, the stage was glutted, a tangle of blood

Patsy Cline

Tonight, I am walking in the pinewoods with a boy who will not look at me, but who holds my hand as if I am his dear dog lunging against restraint, fighting his hold up on hind legs, pulling toward a street of busy traffic

The boy says, *This is where we fell in love,* and I ask, *Who?* because he is a stranger, and then he says, *When you hear that the missing girl's body has been found in the woods, these are the woods you will always see*

He expresses, hand-over-heart, an ache for the loss of these trees, says how he never knew how much he loved the pinewoods until he left, and returned, and left again, and then felt an absence core a clean emptiness in his heart, so he was hollowed and seedless

Seedless, he says, and then a racoon ambles from between the dark trunks of the trees, climbs the boy's clothes, and begins working her way back down, button-by-opened-button, pausing to lift his heart from his chest and slice it into a dozen crescent cuts of white moon

With her nimble hands, what comes next is the racoon making a pie crust butter kneaded into flour until a rough crumb texture is achieved, crumb like crumble, like fall apart, like fall to pieces, which is a song that I can hear playing soft and clear in the distance

And this is a bad dream and a ghost story too, because certain music is equivalent to certain men, and because there is a dead man who would shuffle through the cast-off pine needles with rocking-horse-hips, tilt his head toward the music and say, *They're playing my song—*

*

The funeral parlor in town kept a monkey on a chain in its formal sitting room, and I believed it was a baby, because it wore a diaper, and at a memorial with no viewing, I held a cold can of pineapple soda clear from the reach of its tiny hands while it drank

Because there is little nice to say about my father, what people will say upon his death instead, is how I resemble him, though it isn't really so: we are both contained in bodies that carry their weight badly, and we are both gap-toothed, and we are both easily flushed

But I am not my father's image, or even what could be called a likeness—just a girl who runs toward fat as he was a boy who ran toward fat, soft bodied and mottled, blood too close to the surface of the skin, we two, like shelled creatures shucked

In my step-grandmother's formal dining room there were plaster grapes in a woven cornucopia that she dusted every day, and every day she asked, *How come if raisins is grapes, anyone can have a box of raisins, but grapes is so expensive?*

In the formal dining room, never used, but admired and dusted every day, my step-grandmother hung pictures of her thirteen children, and included those brought to her through marriage, so there was a photograph of my father as a boy, the only one I have ever seen of him as a child

What seems more significant than anything else, our closest link father-to-daughter, is that we were children who had a monkey in common, that he too would have believed it was a baby and kept the cold can just clear of its reach while tipping sips of soda between its thin lips

Deadeye

I will continue to sharpen these stones until all are brought to a point.

Fire Season

Twenty-five miles away, a fire is burning. This is a distance far enough that I need not worry the fire will reach me, but a distance close enough that its smoke does. I am touched by it, as it touches everything I cannot clearly see, obscuring the mountains and warping the sun. Yesterday, the sky was dirty green and the light a steady neon red—a color I have never seen in nature and closed the blinds against. Yesterday, a dove flew, not into the window glass, but with full force into the cinderblock wall. Above the windows I had hung strips of tin foil to interrupt the clean illusion of nothingness, to say, *This is not air.* I could not think that there would ever be a need to announce a cinderblock wall, to say, *This is not air.*

A new day, and I step past the dead dove to put out shallow pans of water for the wild rabbits. On a different day, we would be neighbor-enemies, and I would instead put out little muslin bags of crushed red pepper to keep them from the herbs I am growing despite a drought. But today, the wild rabbits are dying of thirst, and I have water. The former sheriff of this county, a father of five, would take long walks in the desert, looking for caches left for people crossing. On camera, for his campaign, he would flick open his pocket knife and puncture the jugs of water he found, saying, *I am enforcing the law.*

I let the dove's body lay, desiccating in the heat, until two cactus wrens begin to peck at its chest, then one another, fighting for the right to eat. Outside, the heat is gritted with smoke. I clap my hands to drive the wrens away. With a set of tongs and a plastic grocery bag, I collect the dove's body and then toss it all into the special outdoor trash kept exclusively for dog shit.

Hungers

Once, the woodpile cat, feral, with a nest of kittens hidden somewhere there in the splintery dark, tried to take my eye out

I was crouched looking into the jumbled black, into the puzzle of two cords of cut pine dumped from a truck, trying to catch her eyeshine, to see if I could stack my arms full with wood for the fire when a wrong piece pulled could be the cat's little family crushed

She came like I always knew the monster under the bed would come: a reshaping of the dark, a live bolt, quick, as they say, as lightning, which can seem so slow, a tentacle of lavender static stretching to see how much sky it can touch

She raked a fist worth's of dollhouse–sized sickle-curved claws across my eye, cutting through the lid—a sting you can try to imagine

There were snakes in the woodpile too, not poisonous, but who would bite, and my brother, elder, boy, boss of my life, would use a penny knife to cut an X over each, bringing my hand to his mouth, sucking hard, then coughing clear the thin spit-blood, and saying, *Now you owe me, sister*

In the background, our mother, cold in a fake silk robe, only wanted the fire started, the room to warm, the warm hold of the hands of sleep to take her up and carry her down into the dark where all there was, was nothing to see

I want a chimney that exhales hearts like in the drawings little girls make of houses

I will be grateful for the taste of smoke in the air, a screen door to breathe in the bracing spring, the spare mentholated sigh of winter collapsing inward, and a porch where the dog can lay in a band of sunlight dreaming, limp with simple pleasure

And nothing is wrong here, nothing is fraught, no one in earshot is angry or weeping

And I will wash the dishes, which will never wash themselves, dry them with a clean cloth, and put them each in their place on the kitchen shelves

And I will put on water to boil for coffee or for tea, which is to say that whatever I have in the future, I have to share: the sunlight, the wood smoke, the screen door, the spring air, the porch, the dreaming dog

And here, you can trust me with all of your infirmities

I know kitten-fat cats and culling litters, the angry touch of the pretty, bruised-up babysitter, landlocked bodies of shallow, rust-flaked water with cars rotting in their shadowed bellies, mosquitos and mayflies in the lashes of the children's eyes, the colander-eyes of the red-eyed flies at the wet white corners of the horses' eyes that roll blank with the thunder

I too, like you, know a variety of hungers

Mothers

At the age that I am now, my mother had already had all the children she ever would—more than she had ever wanted.

In college, I worked with children at a private school that brought in dancers, drummers, and a man in costume jodhpurs, khaki vest, and pith helmet. He carried with him two canvas sacks: one full of baby alligators, their slender jaws bound with black electrical tape, the other heavy with a docile python dozing looped and looped upon herself inside.

The children were deposited in the mornings by lean, late-teen girls with watercolor eyes and dishwater hair. Many of them were German, part of an exchange program. They released the small hands of small boys and pointed toward wooden chests of brightly colored wooden cars, whispering, "*Auto, auto*," and as a child would step away a girl would step away—one moving forward, the other back, a steady, mutual separation.

The mothers sometimes came in the afternoons in slim-cut suits and calf-straining heels, hair styled and silver-shot. Science had intervened on their behalf and their babies came in sets like gag gift mittens: three to a pair, because one's likely to be lost.

Sometimes the would-be-mothers lost a fetus selectively, sometimes at the recommendation of their doctors, sometimes upon request. *When you pay*, one put it, *you want what you pay for.* Quality versus quantity. I have a theory that this is a style of life most easily maintained by those who have experienced limited want left unfilled. I, though the comparison is poor, will eat all the ice cream set before me, even after my stomach aches, even after I feel the sweetness as a pain in the hinges of my jaw. Bought and paid for—all things put to their full use.

On a Sunday at sunset, I walked with my mother down a raw new road to look at construction going-up, small rock-faced mansions filling a field where we had once, illegally, set loose a calf to graze.

My mother had a new haircut, an angled bob, and a new boyfriend, the developer who had bought the field. He told her she looked like a woman painted by Wyeth, and his hobbies involved helicopters. Freshly harvested, he flew hearts, livers, lungs, and the soft spools of intestines from the bodies of just-dead children for transplant into the bodies of dying ones. His word, *hobby*, to describe this work. *I tell people*, he said, *don't call me a hero*, and later, to my mother, I said, *He wants people to call him a hero*, and she said, *An attitude doesn't alter the outcome of an action.*

Frost was forming over everything, fancy marzipan-pink in the lashes of last light, and the hard new cut of my mother's hair made her face unfamiliar, but she was my mother so I still knew a question forming by the fine, fine wrinkling around her eyes.

She asked what I would do if I found myself pregnant. She was young enough that she might have been, so I drew a finger across my throat, blade-like, *That's what I'd do—*

Voila

Hair scraped back, hands shaking, swallowing, swallowing, asking for water, refusing water, gray, shaking, her hair scraped back, a sour smell, her flesh all filmed in onion-skin-sweat—and a discovery that experience can teach new exhaustion without teaching new expertise.

I give her the bottle, and it's too heavy for her to lift, and she drops it, and it spins spilling water in a clean, wet spiral—pretty—and I pick it up, and I wipe the rim, and I get a little cup, and I pour a little out, and I shape her fingers around the waxed paper, and the shaking in her hand makes the water jump the cup's thin lip before she can raise it to her own, and her quick rise and fall, rise and fall, rise and fall chest is slopped with wet, and so I take the cup before she can drop it, and I hold the back of her neck, and I hold the cup, and I tip water into the open space between her lips, tip and wait, and watch her throat move, tip and wait, and watch her throat move, tip and wait, and watch her throat move, and then use the hem of my shirt to dab around her mouth when the water comes back up, then tip and wait, and watch her throat.

*

Here, I have my two hands hidden behind my back.

You know this game: pick one.

You know this game: you know there's actually something pressed against each palm.

Or, you know a different version: one where each hand is empty.

But, let's go ahead and call this the land of plenty. Both hands closed, neither hand empty, pick one, and the fingers will fold back and *voila*: a prize.

Pick one.

*

Once, I imagined I would be a hundred things. Under the table, on my hands and knees, I played dog, eating from the floor, hoping I might grow up to be a Rottweiler like my best friend with her strong haunches, broad chest, and deep gold eyes.

With a baby doll made all of plastic—Ashleigh was her name—I practiced at being a sailor, a doctor, a mother, a mermaid. I hurled her hollow pink body into the pond behind the house, watched her bob, then plowed after her through cattails and pollywog slog. When I reached her, it was always too late, and then there was a burial at sea, or the straightening of an invisible white coat and stoicism, or grief that could crack bones, or a transformative kiss and Ashleigh's torso fed into a nylon stocking hacked off at the knee, stitched with a sprinkle of sequins—my sweet, pink merbaby.

*

I am a grown woman now, and what I have not become is a dog, a sailor, a doctor, a mother, or a mermaid, and though I trust in my specific skills, still I recognize they are so limited and that many things are better left to that which I am not.

*

When the girl is gone, what stays after is her sick smell, my lurching heart, all the calls to be made ensuring all proper protocol is met.

The next day, smell still hanging, my heart still kicking up, I learn a gang of graduate students, having deputized themselves experts in addiction, have talked the girl out of the formal treatment arranged, and are planning a slumber party weekend wherein they will help their classmate kick while watching underappreciated animated feminist films.

I overhear this in the wide hallway where they are giggling, and gasping, and grasping one another's arms.

Voila.

TIDES

Do you remember—

This is how it begins: my mother with an unfinished question,
rolling her long-boned wrist, the ice in her glass
chasing the track of its confinement

Do you remember—

Is a question with the feel of deep water, which I never feared
until I feared it, and then feared it completely, certain that anything
could be cartwheeling unseen through the cold below,
a fear hatched from the stone egg of a remembered story
I had dug a hole for and hidden and hoped I had forgotten:
a cruel boy who flipped little, bright fish from the shallow water
to the sand to watch them struggle, and then the boy fell from a ship
deep at sea and was forced for ten days to swim,
kept from drowning in the dark and long lapping night
by a creature whose shape was too large to see, and who,
as payment for their protection, took the boy's toes one by one,
and when they were gone, turned to the boy's hands, cleaving each finger
clean from the knuckle bone, leaving the boy on the eleventh morning to crawl,
mauled, across the sand where the little fish had strained for the safety of water

Do you remember—

Is a question that requires I ask a question:

What?

And now my mother says a common woman's name,
belonging to a woman with that name whom I do not know,
but then she names a brother of my father, a man I have not seen
since childhood, an uncle who tossed me high above his head

and caught me with hands always dusted in dried blood,
a farmer, and a builder, and a butcher, a man always broken open
about the knuckles, whom I loved best of all the uncles,
because he loved best my most beloved, the girl cousin in whose arms I slept
safe for my earliest years, her cold fingertip tracing the shell of my ear
as she sang me long, made-up songs about wild horses who
might have been unicorns, eating rosehips unbothered by their thorns,
and then my mother says this woman was my uncle's first wife,
his child bride, a teenaged girl he married with a weedy black-eyed-susan
pinned at his collar when he was a teenaged boy, and then my mother says
my uncle beat his bride so badly, that her pretty face was ruined,
punch after punch pushing the rounded pearls of her teeth
through the pink skin of her cheeks, and forcing her pretty face
to uncenter, all her pretty features smeared into new shape,
like when a word written in the sand is lapped over by a weak wave
that partially consumes it without washing it all the way away,
and then my mother says, *You're lucky for how I've protected you*

In the story I cannot forget, it is the cruel boy's father
who finds him crawling over the sand, and when he sees
that the boy has lost his fingers and lost his toes,
when he sees that his son will never stand upright
on a pitching deck and pull hand-over-hand a slick net
of sequin-scaled fish flipping like silver coins
from the safety of the water into the breathlessness of the air,
the father finds there is no softness in his heart for this child,
that his heart is now barnacled and black toward the boy,
and so the father heaves his once-son into his arms and drops
the boy into a small boat pushed out to sea on the retreating tide

Possibilities

The truth is that death had not occurred to me as a possibility, though I am always saying, *Everyone dies,* as preparation against future loss. Petting the puppy the college girls next door adopted on a whim, delighting in the folds of skin laying loose around its body, I have looked into its sweet eyes and said, *Everything dies, and that is okay; you will grow old and turn white at the muzzle, and you will die, and that is okay.*

Though I am always saying, *Everyone dies,* grown from the hard seed of a child who interred dead pets in cairns of shale, thanking them for the company of their lives, saying, *I am sad that you are dead, but everything dies, and that is okay,* as I kissed and laid the final stone, it had not occurred to me that death was a possibility for the man who has died.

Without knowing anything, I thought I knew everything there was to know, believing that having known the man once, I knew him still, imagining him living the same life that I had shared, believing he would carry on that way for so long as I was alive: joint-ends and midnight swims, the blades of his browned shoulders breaking the water as he pulled himself through the reflection of the moon on the lake, every morning waking too early, turning toward the ghost of a loon's cry and then drifting through empty, unused rooms, past a weight bench in the place of a dining table, but with his mother's prized pink china poodles still displayed on the sideboard.

I did not live with the man in his house on the lake, which had been his parents before it was his, but I was left there—my mother hospitalized, my father untrustworthy—for a period of time long enough that the man and I developed our own domesticity. What is intimacy, if not knowing the state of a person's bathroom when nothing has been tidied for company? A cabinet half-full of brown bottles of half-empty tanning accelerators and crumpled tubes of skin creams, the heavy white smell of Embryolisse—which all the French, he said, swore by—and the heavy sweet smell of fake coconut, and his big handprint greasing the gilt mirror.

Every morning, he made me black tea, half steeped, worried the caffeine would corrupt my growing bones, though every night he let me sit in his lap to watch slashers, movies of men murdering women with knives, bursting into their white-frilled bedrooms again and again, each stab at a taunt, tanned midsection powered by a thrust of the killer's hips.

Some afternoons, I floated on my back in the lake stroking the smoothness of my belly. Some afternoons, I sat in the shallows in the shade of a pine and studied the man at play with one woman or the other, arms around one another's shoulders, or a woman's legs around his waist. I liked the way long hair spread on the water, and the mystery of the possibilities occurring underneath.

When the confrontation between two of the women came, the man pulled me by the wrist from the floral chaise where I slept, hefted me on his hip, pushed my head to his shoulder, and told the women they had to leave: just look, just look, he said, at what they were doing to me, frightening a frightened little girl.

I did think I could be a child bride. The first great crisis of my life: did I want this man as a father or a lover? Choices are easier when there are none, and there is nothing new here. Turn over mulch and there may be maggots, but here, there is no new life to find: a bad man can be good to animals and children and still be a bad man.

Birdsong

What birdsong?

Night is still running her gray laps, and I know my mouth
cages teeth, because in sleep they bite at one another.
Full of bruises and white mice, I listen for the ghost
of the sound of a spoon stirring sugar into coffee.

For years, I woke in my childhood bed choking on terror,
begging to go home. Disorientation is the familiar now
when I open my eyes to an unfamiliar room. The ant-fight
light from a television across the hall crawls over a set
of green and yellow foo dogs in a bow-legged curio cabinet.

This is my grandmother's house. Her mother, before marriage,
toured China by motorcycle, the breasts of a piano teacher,
a lover, pressed to her back. Under one paw, the male foo dog
pins a ball, a symbol of the earth. The other, the female of the pair,
holds nothing, but is harried by a long-clawed cub climbing her chest.
This too must be symbolic, but my knowledge is limited
to the littlest bit I know: the ball, the earth.

A re-enactment of an encounter with a swamp monster
is playing at an uncomfortable volume on the television. I cannot
not listen as actors in the role of deer hunters say they are feeling watched
and then their hound yips and then goes silent.

Puppies, how they seek the nipple when their eyes are still sealed—
This is how I find my grandmother, one breast
slipped from the armhole of her nightgown and dangling,
as she gropes her way down the hall to the kitchen for more sweet, pink wine.

I say her name.
I have always only called her by her name.

What I have inherited and what I have not: she is pale,
gold-freckled, long-limbed, a tall, handsome woman. I stand
level with the base of her throat. To straighten her clothes,
I am reaching up. I am reaching up to straighten her nightgown,
to pull the armhole away from her body, to scoop her breast
into my palm and ease it back through the gap.

Hatched from an egg, this woman said throughout
my childhood because I resemble no woman from her line.
There was no affection in it: *Hatched from an egg.*
Why sleep again and risk the waking?
I can sit the shift of light, night to day,
from not-silence to wild birdsong,
looking at the darker skin of my hand
on the paler skin of my breast.

Balance

There are certain stories I want to tell, but
am hesitant to tell for how fully they will reveal me
and those that I have loved. In the first part of life,
I was mothered most by another child, a girl-relative
close to my own age, but already wary as a stray:
a watcher of hands and quick-footed. A girl I understood
to protect me, though I did not understand from what,
a testament to her dedication. Lighting the morning
fire, I had burned a fingertip on the still hot head
of an extinguished match and had not stopped sulking
over the small and pulsing red bite of pain, treating
the hurt hand as if I had been made to hold a hot coal
under torture and nobly endured. *I am hurt*, I said. *I am hurt.*
All morning: *I am hurt. Look. I am hurt.* The girl took me outside,
where salvaged lumber was dumped onto itself in a pile of points
and angles, and dragged a nail-pierced board free from the rest.
Walk this like a balance beam, she said, and because she was
my greatest love, my little mother, I arranged myself
heel-to-toe, arms out like a gymnast for balance, and stepped forward—
Under my weight, the first nail punched through the toughened sole
of my foot, pushed, pushed, and pushed all the way through
blooming as a wide blown blood poppy, a flower in a poem
about to lose its petals: red, black centered, and reaching.
What worries me about telling this story is that others
will not understand that this was not a lesson the girl wanted
to teach, but taught regardless for my benefit, because she knew
what I had not yet learned, kept ignorant in her care:
nothing would stop for my small hurts, and there would be worse
wounds, truer than the nip from a match-coal that bubbled-up a blister,
and these would raise concern from no one. Can a reader understand:
the necessity of knowing, early in life, that no one would pity me
for a pain I caused myself through carelessness, and that it was time too,
before it was too late to safely learn, to learn to expect care from no one.

Tooth Box

A keep-safe for a keep-sake of a child,
a fragile capsule for caging time.
Made of milk-thin porcelain that
a careless hand could put a thumb through,
the box on the dresser top, painted with a
red-eyed rabbit and bordered with a line
of gold so old it has rubbed away in places,
worried by fingertips or years, or fingertips and years,
and at night, its blue-white-translucence becomes
soft light, and who knows whose mother
may have carried it across what wet black sea full
of monsters and through what wet black forest full
of men ready to murder any they encountered.

Is it true, or a story, or a story built from the sticks
and bleached and brittle bones of a truth died and
scattered, that fur trappers would string up rivals
in makeshift sacks shaped from poor-quality skins and
light a fire underneath to serve a slow, long-suffering death?

On the pond where we skated in tight figure-eights,
pretending we were the mechanical girl in a music box,
underneath the hardened skin of milk-white ice
that we pretended was a cut of mirror simulating ice,
a man had set snare traps for the beavers,
and we fished them up and swung them
between us—*one for the money, two for the show,
three to get ready, four to go*—
and team-work tossed them deep into the
blackberry brambles to save the animals a slow death
by drowning, noosed cold under the water that was their home.

Our step-grandmother, with her peaked aubergine brows
and red-black mouth—*draw up,* she said, at the mirror—
lift the face and pick one feature to feature—
would sit on the bed that had been her sister the nun's,
when her sister the nun had been brought home to die,
where we lay still like skeletons under white sheets
ironed, starched stiff, pulled over our shoulders and
tucked tightly around us, and our step-grandmother
would tell us stories about girls who had become animals
to save themselves, the hot blood blanket of a skin
so new to death it heaved and shuddered
across the thin back it concealed:
Donkey Skin, and Porcupine Skin,
and Seal Skin, and Horse Skin—girls,
like we were girls, transformed to undesirable,
or untouchable, too slippery, or too fast to catch.

When the man who set the snares came across us,
he carried with him a pipe laid over his shoulder like a club—
to finish, I am certain, any killing the wire nooses had not.
Hey, and he came fast through the tall frozen grass,
the blades chiming ice-skin against ice-skin—*hey, you
dumb little bitches, you dumb little cunts, I'll feed you
your fucking teeth.*

We had been taught danger, the white flag
of a doe's tail, in deer, the signal to flee,
in men, the signal of surrender. We had been
taught first flight and then to shelter, concealed,
the safety of a sister's-pinky playing mother's-nipple
in the baby's mouth to keep it from crying out,
from giving away the hiding place of the helpless.

What scared me most was not the man, how he
came at us in violence, but how the girl beside me,
in response, knelt and wrenched a skate from her foot,
and shoving up, held it blade-out ready to slash or stab,
ready to fight, and how after all my little life of us
side-by-side, two, the girls, the same, a set, nature's
made match, she was another thing entirely.

Was

I was, I thought, just a kid,
and though she had done her best
to give me some childhood in our shared years,
she made clear that that was all over,
and it was time to repay the debt
I had accrued. So, I barked at her about boys
with nothing but bad luck potential.
My god, I said, a little fishwife, a little nag,
a little fake mother who shivered and sweat
at the idea of the word cumming—
the raw, humiliating curve of the letter u,
hanging like a spit slick tit—
a little sunburnt pig, too prim to roll in the mud,
a little box of self-hate tied tidy with a bow,
readying myself for a future of misery
and hag-dom with a husband I had not met,
had not even cast apple pips into the fire to predict.
Do you have to go out every night?
In books about brutal crimes,
I am always moved by the author's compulsion
to explain that no photo can do the dead girl justice,
can capture her, because her beauty was a living thing.
It's 4:17, she said, *in the afternoon. I could go out
for an hour and still get an early bird supper,*
and she left, and did not come back that night.
After four days, I powered-on the dense gray block
of the outdated computer, listening to the robot-warble
of the dial-up modem and in less than five minutes
found her booking photo and learned she had been picked-up
for underage drinking three counties away.
The phone connection, when we spoke, was weak.
I asked, *When will you come home?*
And she answered, *When I can.*
I worried every time I saw her
would be the last, but it never was,
until it was.

The Right Word

Is it irony that is lost on my mother,
when she kills a red squirrel for raiding
the nest a pair of house finches
has built above her door
on the same day she butchers
the thirty-four dumb white chickens
she has raised from damp
and freshly hatched, to shore up
the meat store in her cellar's casket freezer?
I know, she says, *everyone has to eat*,
tossing the squirrel's limp body
overhand into the pinewoods,
where she hopes the dogs
will not sniff it out to roll in,
but I hate nature. On the lawn
behind her, the tools of the day,
washed clean of blood and the mysteries
of the avian body, are drying in the sun:
a cleaver, and a pair of kitchen shears,
and an orderly line of metal killing cones,
which look like nothing but funnels,
unless you know, like I know,
that they are used to hold poultry
upside down, immobile and disoriented,
in a state called toxic euphoria,
which renders them still and silent,
no flapping of wings or squawking,
to more easily cut their throats.

Kindness

I never had the lead, but always had lines and often a moment alone on the stage in the high school plays. I could dance a decent box step while belting out a tune and could be counted on to deliver Shakespeare cleanly. Not talented, but competent, reliable, and I was pleased with myself to be a girl who would not spook or showboat in the spotlight's moony stare.

Our home-economics teacher, who served as the director, had been an actress in Hollywood when she was young and still pretty, before a bad marriage, and two-out-of-three addict kids, appearing in a scene in a famous movie for long enough that anyone who knew her could pick her out from the crowd of extras moving on the street.

In rehearsals, she liked to demonstrate seduction: *Got a light?* the orange leather of her décolletage pressed to a boy's arm, until one showed his chops, performing perfect theatrical revulsion, leaping back, pop-eyed, quivering hands held out to shield himself from her purr and slinky touch.

To me, that same day, she said, *Look, you're a good girl, but that's it.* And I knew it was meant as a kindness from a woman not particularly skilled at being kind, but was insulted that she thought I needed to be told I was not special, as if sixteen years of life had not taught me that every day for sixteen years.

The boy who all the boys called Nips—nips as in nipples, for the color, and texture, and staggering size of the zits obliterating any beauty he might have had—was watching the exchange and when it was done, tilted his head toward the side door and together we slipped out, unseen, into a sunset.

We did not go and get high, or go and fuck in the ugly hide-a-way of the gravel pit, tearing up our skin on rocks with a beautiful, unreachable candy-color sky above us. We walked to a mom-and-pop shop that sold live bait, and penny candies, and fancy sandwiches for tourists to take to the beach, and convinced the woman working the register to give us the last of the chili from lunch. She was readying to scrape it into the trash, and let me drag the pot sides with the ladle and slop what I could into a bag of corn chips we had bought.

Outside, it was already dark, though barely supper time. Even with the sun shuttered, the boy's face was malformed, pulped at its edges, the dark-on-dark shadows falling wrong. I had made it, always, a point to call him by his name rather than use the nickname he allowed, and squinting, trying to bring his features into a smooth order they would not take, I wanted to apologize for my club-handed kindness, that despite all its good intentions, asked for more than it gave, but I knew that would have only made it worse.

BITES

No-see-ums, smaller than a mouse dropping brushed from the butcher's block, smaller than a seed of black sesame, small enough to slip, unseen, through the rusted square of a window screen's metal mesh, caught on an eyelash, touch-light, like a snowflake's settling, the smallest shock of sensation, thrumming, the beating of tiny wings, the beating of tiny feet against the tensile of a hair until the tiny body, too small for sight, tears itself apart—

There are so many things to keep us awake at night, so many mouths eating at our rest until all that is left is the final bite, too large to finish, but not worth saving. Throw it to the dog.

I think the history of any coast is a story of being eaten alive by your own mother. I think of the castaways at sea who joined a lottery to be cannibalized when rescue did not come. I think of what I have learned about scenarios of extreme dehydration: that you are better off drinking blood than urine. I think of the couple who, before I was born, went for a jeep ride in The Sahara with their small son, became stranded, strangled the child to end his suffering, then opened his body and drank his blood.

I think of my father, who when the cat leapt into my lap at the supper table, grabbed it by the tail and slung it, as hard as he could, against the wall, then went back to cutting his pork chop. I think of my mother sitting across from me, saying coolly, *Don't cry,* then sipping from a tall gin and tonic, and I think of the cat dragging its deadened leg.

I do not know, yet, if I am bitten. I cannot feel, yet, if the lid of my eye will swell, turn dark and wet-fleshed as a plum.

Tomorrow, I will gather with students in a circle under the faint and constant thrum of a bank of florescent lights, and we will talk about associative movement in writing and how it mirrors the function of memory. Of the ending of a story we have all read, I will ask, *How did we get here?* I do not know, yet, if they will ask, *What happened to your eye?*

Wolves

Hold that horror image: the horse on its hind legs, folding as it falls, eyes rolled back white

*

Now, I take a small sampling of white pills, not so many, but more than before, which was none

*

Delivered quick, like a hammer to the temple swung from a clear blue sky, I am prepared for the gut drop, the television screen turning klaxon red, the nauseating slur of my going-sluggish blood, the cold stumble as it slows, the brass horns fading out into the oratory of a reporter, solemn in his bright tie, announcing death tolls, saving always, the children for last

*

A dead child, the cherry on top of the sad shit sundae of the day

*

I have seen people who seem to me the very best of parents, the ice cream sundae with a cherry on top of parents, and still their children are too wounded by their mother's eyes, by their father's eyes, to meet their parents' eyes at the dinner table

*

I have a dream where I am sitting vigil at the deathbed of the son I have not had

He is an old man who recognizes the end of his life as more natural than awful

I am proud of his openness to death, that he is not sad, or frightened, or angry, only the littlest bit impatient, as if he's missed the green light and is sitting, again, through the traffic cycle

Then he asks me for a glass of water, *Water, please*, but there's no water left on Earth

Water, he says, *please* and then *Please, water*, but in my dream there's no water left on Earth

*

Mama, he says, and dies, betrayed

*

On the first day of class, on the roster, I am making little notes: Margaret who is a Polly, Alberto, who is a Tito, Lenora, who invites the room to call her what her mother does, which is Lo, which I love the mouthfeel of, saying to myself again and again: *Lo, Lo*

And next is a girl with a headband with cat ears holding back dyed black hair

I'm a wolf, she says, *born in human form*

*

History loves its feral children, wolf-boys who don't shiver in the snowy mountains, wolf-girls who don't sweat striped in wet jungle shadows, babies with their baby teeth filed to fine points, little hands curled into calloused clubs, blood around the rosebud mouth

My pencil hovers—*Identifies as wolf*—

But this, I will remember without help

*

Held in memory, a blurred and reddish photograph: a tiny form protected by the sickle moon curve of a mother-wolf, but if the memory is turned, examined from all angles. touched in the dark of the mind, the textures are wrong, and what appears a girl, isn't a girl

Instead, glass eyed and sawdust stuffed, a real girl's borrowed doll fails to hold a pose, and the wolf, I think, is a dead thing too, its body curled to fake compassion

*

And I am afraid, in this moment, pencil hovering—*Identifies as wolf*—

*

Scientific research supports that for humans, as for wolves, communal living was essential to our rise: together we reared our young more effectively, more effectively, together, we hunted and we killed

*

I am afraid not so much of the moth-eaten ozone, or the instability of my career, or the sons I will never be fit for, or the odd boy in all black in summer at the back of the room with the limbs of a disarticulated doll dangling from his backpack, or even the fields of ice turning to water and creeping toward the coast while polar bears swim and swim and swim

*

I am afraid of being participant in a world that makes people want to forsake their humanity and throw themselves to the wolves, as if the wolves will welcome them, as if the wolves won't bite

FIDDLEHEAD

A person someone else might call a friend, but who I'll not, not because of any action on any person's part, but because I have only known him distantly, and years ago, when he could still write about teenage rage because of its adjacency to what was then his current age, has recently had a second son and now writes to limited acclaim about the smell of his small boys and the uncurling of fiddlehead ferns, an edible plant I have gathered with my mother at the edge of a frothy river below a papermill where signs with a leaping fish circled and cut through—*Unsafe for Consumption*—were posted along the bank.

Now, I see fiddleheads sold in the chicest of the chic grocery stores where I touch everything, but buy very little, piled high and living-green behind a purple lettered chalkboard reading *Wild Harvested*. The temptation is to put my hands in them, to root down elbow deep into their display and lay my cheek to their tight green curls and whisper, *Oh baby—how far you've come.*

I think we all endure a panoply of pure and painful things at each turn of each moment of each day of each one of all of our lives. We round-the-corner on a pearl-gray morning full of soft dove song and walk into the stiff-armed punch of a clown, who observes our bloodied nose and shakes a fat white gloved finger—*uh, uh, uh*—in reprimand then turns and bowleg-bobbles at startling speed down the sidewalk in squeaking, oversized, red shoes.

I was not afraid of clowns, but of adults and china dolls behaving unpredictably when night granted temporary permission for actions impossible or unacceptable during daylight. Believing either—adult or doll—might cut my throat in the dark, I slept uneasy, hands wound around my neck, the blanket pulled over my head.

The person who someone else might call a friend, but who I'll not, not
because of any action on any person's part, but because I have only
known him distantly, and years ago when he could still write about
teenage rage because of its adjacency to what was then his current
age, is not so well received as he once was, it seems because, what was
identified as his signature sizzle, his abundant anger, is absent now,
muted with time—time, which is change—to melancholy, a somber
near-silence as saturating as the purple smell of lilacs after rain,
with this new heaviness on rare occasion exchanged for the arguable
generosity of sharing a moment of dazzled contentment.

Pearls

My great grandmother did not warn me about the alligator in the canal, who had three days before, pulled a girl from a swim ladder into its dark water. Instead, she gave me a child's net made from delicate blue mesh, its handle topped with a star, and said, *Go wade off the boat launch and see if you can catch Grammie any little fishes.*

At night, I slept in my great grandmother's vast white room, double beds with a low white wicker hutch shared between them, paintings of women in white dresses standing in the sand dunes at the shore on the white walls, and a white umbrella cockatoo dancing on the wooden bar in the gold bell of his cage. She said, *If you can catch some little fishes we'll put them between us in the punch bowl, and they'll look like swimming sprinkles of stars, and we can watch them until we fall asleep and then have mermaid dreams.*

I was not an orphan. My mother and her mother, who lived with her mother, my great grandmother, in the long white house of windows on the canal, were out together, buying pearls. At a famous jeweler's they were paying to play a game of chance. It worked like this: you gave a man your money then picked an Akoya Oyster from a tank in the center of the showroom, and it was split in front of you for the pearl inside.

A prize. Or, it might be something piddling squeezed from the soft gut, a little sphere with a little shine only appropriate for a piece of jewelry for a child, and then you could have your hard little bead of disappointment set on the nose of a gold charm in the shape of a seal, balanced there like a ball, and give it to some little girl. But you could get lucky, you could pick the fattest pearl, worth far more than what you had paid, and then the jeweler would sit you in a nacre-gray velvet chair and sketch a custom setting under your direction, anything pre-made too small to hold the moon you had pulled from the stomach of the sea.

Put them back, my great grandmother said, when I held out to her the plastic cup of tiny bright fish, translucent with shining silver bones, that I had netted from the canal's dark water. *Put them back right now.*

At dinner, my mother wore a delicate gold chain with a gold charm shaped like a scallop's shell, a pearl set in its center. *You look like a tourist*, my great grandmother said. She wore all white: a white linen tunic over white linen pants, white sandals, white pearls in her ears. She looked from my mother to my grandmother. They were both tall and long legged, women with long thighs perfumed with white powder on whom dresses were always short. *You look cheap*, my great grandmother said, and then the meal was delivered by a quartet of silent, synchronized waiters in white. Whatever had been ordered for me had a bone protruding, meat styled so a bone stood straight as the wooden bar in the gold bell of the cockatoo's cage.

My great grandmother's eyes touched my plate and slid up. It was a rule to look at her when she looked at you. Manners must be minded. My hands were in my lap, waiting for her permission to touch what was set on the table. I did not want whatever clung to the bone, but my pink and effervescent drink, yes. The maraschino cherry stuck through with a pink cocktail umbrella, bleeding sweet red syrup, yes. *Three days ago,* my great grandmother said, and told how an alligator in the canal had pulled a girl from a swim ladder into its dark water, then held her under to drown her, though the girl had not drowned, had only had one leg mangled so badly that when she was fought from its teeth there was nothing but bone below her thigh, and then my great grandmother said to me, *Eat.*

Wonders

In the desert plants are tough-skinned, thorny, armored and spiked, designed for self-protection, evolved to keep their soft innards safe, to guard the precious liquid there, narrow bands of flowing moisture scientists have recorded with specialized microphones, capturing a slow pulsing not unsimilar to the push of blood through the human body.

Soundtracks of such living things can be bought in stores that sell tasseled ottomans and red currant candles in hobnob glass, tree of life wall tapestries, and lace bralettes with dozens of intersecting straps.

A bird's beak is a spike of sorts. A rat's teeth, a version as well. The black snake, which can appear matte, flat, without gloss, turns bedazzled when struck by the sun and can be longer than a man is tall and is beloved because it will kill a rat and eat it, and then the rat will not eat its way into the cacti that bloom so prettily in an otherwise empty gravel yard.

In nature, there are many things designed for the undoing of other things, and many things have learned, on top of these natural gifts, specialized arts of undoing.

A seagull, having scooped a sideways-skittering crab from the shallow safety of the water, will carry it up until the gull is only wings, the v of a child's drawing against the blue background of the sky, and then, as it passes over the jag of a seaside cliff, release its catch to crack the crab open on the rocks below.

In the damp places in the northeastern forests, in the laved, low-lying places where leaf litter degrades back toward dirt, places where darkness is freckled by light, places black with stagnant moisture and maroon smells, golden mushrooms grow, delicately stemmed and with a jaunty frilled cap: the treasured chanterelle and its toxic sister, the false chanterelle, which are nearly identical in appearance. The first is protected against harvest by the second, and so both live and thrive.

Assisted by of an unguent made from the entrails of a sacrificed infant, reports recount that a witch might insert a broom handle into the anus of a goat allowing it to carry sixteen children to their sabbath, where, upon arrival and unloading of its passengers, the goat would remove the broom handle to play the flute and dance upright by the light of the witches' fire.

In nature, there are designs that seem cruel. Why are elephants, for example, given the capacity of memory necessary to cross great swaths of changing land and also an understanding of loss? Why year after year, for a long, long life, must a herd mourn their dead matriarch, mourn first one, then another calf who couldn't take another step toward water, who collapsed and was scavenged upon, eaten until too rotten to eat, and finally left to rot away, only the bones left behind, which each year, are paused over, grief an even greater pull than the need for water, the bones caressed even after they are craggy with age. What is the benefit of an elephant understanding loss?

On the West Coast, a mother claimed her son's teacher would flush her little boy down a toilet into a secret warren of rooms underneath the school where rituals to honor Satan were performed. The youngest students, she said, were sacrificed then consumed raw in orgiastic feasting, the plump pink of a nipple in the mouth replaced by the plump pink of a baby's toe, softness with an afterburn, like an oyster sprinkled with horse radish and swallowed down.

Children, the mother said, were tortured with power drills applied to their armpits. Children dropped off in the morning, the mother said, were spirited away to Mexico in hot air balloons, made to swallow live black snakes and eat fistfuls of feces then brought back and cleaned up just in time for pickup.

How obviously this is ridiculous. But so rich is fear that fathers and mothers descended on the schoolgrounds with shovels and buckets, a backhoe even, digging to prove the impossibility of secret rooms of black candles, black robes, red lights, and red vessels of babies' blood. What did they find? A turtle's shell. The cracked plastic pedal of a tricycle. A plastic snack bag patterned with Mickey Mouse, dragged under the earth by a rat.

Encouraged, they kept digging.

And of course, the mother who made the accusations was insane. Her brain was wild with chemicals out of whack. And she ruined lives, of course she ruined lives, with her wonderous accusations, investigated by authorities for years upon years upon years. And of course, she didn't mean it. Of course. And of course, she didn't understand what she had done. And of course, it could be said that she was a victim too. Of course, that could be said. Of course.

And I could rock myself to sleep to the lullaby of a hate filled heart that truly meant every evil it ever did. I could finally sleep well at night if only every awful story had a villain equally as bad.

O

Dear Enemy,

Imagine I am tracking you through the night with a stocking full of shattered glass to bring down on you from behind, to bring you to your knees, to knock you senseless

Imagine the moon above, one wide, white cataract-ed eye and know the moon doesn't pity you for anything but for your pitted cheeks—like the moment peroxide touches baking soda—and know this is a form of sympathy like the form of delight when people in a movie theatre laugh at the appearance of a brand they once used, now defunct, saying: *Remember that; I remember that*—

Imagine this now too: that even white-out blind, the moon can spot an ugly girl if she's ugly on the inside—it's the pitch of the voice, its taffy pull—and you, Dear Enemy, are, in the ways that count the most, ugly in spades, sugar stretched far too far, the hard candy that cuts the tongue that turns it

And who likes that? You know, I know, everyone knows, because there's nobody who likes that—

Nobody

The ready metaphor, Dear Enemy, for what's wrong with you is cancer, creeping, a dark tentacle binding and blighting your softest purple-greens and retch-provoking reds, all your slick, intimate meat, your offal that hangs in front of you in its slack sack, all of it tied tight with a live black thread of poison

But I will ask you now to imagine instead a rabbit taken fresh from the field, brought to you in its final twitch by a tabby cat whose bloody face you've kissed not even an hour ago

Imagine, Dear Enemy, when you wrench the rabbit away, wanting to save it, to send it hopping back to the high grass, that you feel against your palm the delicate protrusion of a proliferation of blood-thickened ticks all along its filthy belly

Imagine now, Dear Enemy, if you were to take a penny knife, flick open the blade and cut around each quick rabbit-foot, slip the point up under the skin and slice straight and shallow from nether to yon and then work your hand underneath and spread your fingers and make the gap you've opened gape

What you feel, Dear Enemy, I think I know, is everything slick you're afraid of

O—

And the moon sees the empty hole of your mouth, the slack anus where the botfly lays its eggs, and the moon, a body, a blind white eye, a high, round belly, a water-spotted crystal cup of light, a patron of women, a puller, hand-over-fist, of the tides is the witness of what lives on the inside

Imagine, Dear Enemy, that she sees you sprawled and sees through you, and the moon does not pity you

Spirals

Imagine dominoes, not the game that old people play—the *slap-slap* of tiles meeting on a yellow linoleum tabletop, instant coffee, fruit crème sandwich cookies, the lemon pith sourness of sweet Florida Water Cologne poured into the bathwater for fifty years, seeping now from the gentle folds of soft loose skin—but the tiles arranged upright in a pattern, and imagine the pattern is a massive swirl and imagine the swirl is the galaxy—a representation of the galaxy in an Archimedean spiral of dominoes, black and white as an imaginary night sky struck through by stars—and imagine now that the swirl of the galaxy is intended to act as a representation of a narrative structure: see the starting point and how every point, though now disconnected, will, when the tiles neatly fall, illustrate how each act is dependent on what came before to reach where it will next go, all tripping toward an end, all pushed toward an end, and see how the story opens out at a consistent grade, growing larger and larger with each turn, each turn a larger turn than the last turn—see how the spiral spins out and out, but remember its dependence on origin, remember how everything hinges on the first piece put into its position, that every piece after is instructed by the first.

Now, science-museum-style, or on a smaller scale, science-class-style, tip one tile in the mind and watch the upright pattern fall, maintained but remade, as tile fells tile, a flattening, each tile tripping another, pushing another and then the next, another and then the next, and the next and the next and the next, until everything has fallen. One flick and there: it's done.

Now, when a pig is slaughtered, it's bled, its throat slit, but for the sake of humanity toward the animal and for the safety of the people who will repattern the pig, the living thing, into edible cuts of meat, the blade brought across the pig's throat is frequently not the first step, instead, the pig is plugged in the brain, a bite of metal inserted at great force in the pink and blood rippled organ, stifling, if not stopping, stifling the work of nearby sensory organs—sight for example, stifled if not stopped—and there is a tool, a pneumatic gun which looks like a fire extinguisher and is, as described, an extinguisher of sorts, though the word pneumatic—a punch of air, the delivery system for the metal pellet—is derived from the word for breath.

Piggy goes to market and weeks later, piggy comes home, now processed and packaged in white paper. With him, Piggy brings home the bacon, the sausage, the chops, the loins, the roasts. Piggy's becoming: *Behold, I am the other white meat.*

An extinguisher of a living consciousness, if not always an extinguisher of life, the pneumatic gun, the tool, fires, as previously described, a metal plug, a blunt force bullet through the shell of the skull into the softness of the pink and red ripple sherbet of the brain and when the pig is stupefied, it can be hauled up, hung by its rear trotters, throat slit, bled, then butchered. There is the tool, the pneumatic gun, a hissing snag of air and the metal plug pushed deep into the mind, but some people also use what is on hand, and sometimes what is on hand is sometimes a BB gun with its skin-splitting but non-lethal little-boy-pellets—birds alone beware—which men must pump by the dozen into the crown of a substantial skull to try to crack it and silence the screaming inside. Both for mercy and for ease of the work to follow, they do this.

Motivations are not singular.

But say, having loaded a pig into the back of a slat sided truck modified with iron rebar and hooks from which to hang a heavy body, a vehicle for butchering, say, having goaded the pig up the ramp and worked it toward a corner and put a pellet in its brain, say it screams and flails, runs circles round and round the truck bed, not going down, not going silent, just screaming, alive and suffering and loud.

What would anyone do to undo what they've just done, but at this point, there's no point, there's no going back. There's no retraction for a pellet to the brain.

When one domino is tipped all the other tiles should fall and fall and fall spiraling from sound into silence.

The point being: there's one clear conclusion to this narrative. The first sentence has written the last. The point being: don't flick what you don't want to see fall. The point being: don't deliver harm to any thing you would want anything less than dead.

Denouement

I worry about the dead who have died unable to finish the last book they were reading and that they are haunted by questions of a story that has an end they were not able to reach.

*

Though I am the youngest, my eyes are ruined, worse than anyone in the family's, worse than genetics suggest they should be. My greatest fear, nonsensical, like the way a friend is certain she will be framed for murder and sent to prison, her pleas of innocence rejected, her insistence of a conspiracy mocked, is that there will be a disaster in the night on such a scale that I will have to run, weeping, and naked, and terrified, and blind into the street, fire, or the roiling, rainbow bubbles of a toxic spill, or the skin-serrating keratin barbs of a tiger's tongue licking at my back, my glasses left behind, which means I will be useless, except as food, morally obligated to offer myself up for cannibalization, because unaided by a prescription lens, I cannot tell one black and white dog from another, even when they look nothing alike.

*

My father blamed books, reading daily in dull light, for my pathetic eyesight and the expenses associated with a child who, at less than an arm's length, could see only shape and color. Like a stone, I fell from the climbing tree, my fingers closing to grip a branch they only grazed. *Watch it*, my father said, and I stepped straight into the blue tunnel left by an ice auger's bit, dropped from sight under winter water, and was hauled back into the breathing world by a handful of wet hair and the hood of my sodden down jacket. Though I was saved, a winter boot was lost. When the optometrist slipped my first pair of glasses into place, I did not recognize my mother or my brother. I did not know the fine details of their faces: the pale, apricot freckles high on my mother's cheeks, the golden stripe through my brother's blue eye. My father looked no different. I knew him, as I always would: by his squat bulk, his mean, boiled redness.

*

Above our heads, in the walled off loft, grew a Jurassic jungle of marijuana, my father a small-town dealer with grand plans to be a northeastern kingpin. He lived in a paranoid terror of discovery and capture, certain the police surveilled all his movements: the to-and-fro from the fridge for another glass of milk, the way he unbuckled his belt and opened his fly before reclining in his chair, eyes closed, smoking a joint pinched in the metal jaws of a hemostat.

*

My mother worked an overnight shift at the regional hospital. She sat at the front desk directly through the emergency room doors, trying to gather information from men who staggered in with tuna hooks through their hands, the wicked barb fighting all attempts at removal. On worse nights, she watched men, blood softly spurting from a wedged wound where a chainsaw had kicked back and cut deep, be carried in terrifyingly limp. Then she bashed at the red button that rang into the room where the on-call doctor slept, then used the intercom to request a janitor with a mop and bleach. On the worst night, a frantic girl, her own age thereabouts, came wailing through the doors and thrust a baby over the desk into my mother's arms, and the moment she took its tiny weight, she knew the baby was dead, but still the baby's mother was screaming, *Help me! Oh, help me!* and in my mother's arms, the baby's body was like a bag, she said, of broken chips, and she knew, knew like she always knew when the neighbor boys were hiding, watching her hang the laundry in her bikini, knew the screaming mother had shaken the baby, had dashed the baby against the wall, had hurled the baby to the floor. *Like a bag of broken chips,* she said, sitting in the dark, at the edge of my bed, my stuffed deer—weak necked, long legged, and grubby—a tangle in her lap. And, I, a baby still, just two or three, reached out, touched her hand, and asked with all sincerity, *Can I have a chip?*

*

The police, my father said, *know what to look for.* A man I thought of as an uncle would call collect with a bad connection, his voice wrapped in a vibrating gray sound as if he was dialing from inside a hive of wasps. Under the curved roof a Quonset hut filled with light and dripping water, he had kept a Jurassic jungle too, but had not thought to offset the power usage of banks of grow lights. *That's how they got him*, my father said. *His power bills.* At night, after my mother left for work, we did not use electricity in the house, except in the loft, where special lights operated on twelve-hour timers, ensuring the jungle's rapid growth. In the living room, there was a set of antique oil lamps with tall, thin glass chimneys. I would lay on the floor below their soft, smoky light, my cheek to the page of a book.

*

I have always loved dioramas, but the unfinished book left by a reader who finished everything, haunted me. The water glass, three-quarters full on the floor at the bedside, its rim overlapped with pink imprints where a glossed mouth had kissed, I wanted to keep just as it was forever, but the book, like cupped hands, like wings, its spine cracked and covers facing upward, was intolerable. What I have always wanted is a cabinet of taxidermied terns, posed nesting in shallow divots dug below the seagrass, painted waves unfolding behind them, one strung with wires to simulate flight. I have imagined pushing a button to activate a recording of beach sounds and bird calls, and how it would feel for my bones to soften, my body to become give, the hard floor turning to sand because I would be sinking. In a dream, I broke the frozen moment, cracked its stand-still-mirror-stare. I opened the case and cut one of the wires keeping the gliding tern suspended in air.

One was enough. Twisting at an unnatural angle on the remaining wire, any illusion of life captured in the cabinet was ruined. It was so obvious: everything was dead.

*

When a person leaves life suddenly, they are both absent and present. In a book, the younger sister moves through the older sister's house, tracing again and again a mark on a stair which might have come from moving furniture, or from a struggle. She touches everything, but changes nothing. The final chapter dedicates itself to the younger sister's decision to throw away a bowl of tomatoes turned to gray pulp, fogged by hundreds of tiniest flies. They are symbolic tomatoes. In the end the older sister's disappearance remains unsolved. The younger sister returns to her own life, and in three years, has a baby, a daughter, and chooses, in the final line, not to name the infant girl for her dead sister.

*

In graduate school, a professor asked the girls from her class to dress in loose white sheets and serve wine at the party for her book's release. *You will*, she said, *be naiads*. Drifting silent through groups of chatter, holding a decanter around its thin glass throat, I thought I was more evocative of a ghost. As a gesture of thanks, the professor later invited us to her house for what she described as a *special treat*. Pizza, I thought, or small, fancy cakes, but it was instead a woman who claimed psychic abilities and arrived with an elderly chihuahua under her arm, her first business to take a white, plastic backed pad from her purse and spread it on the floor so the tiny dog could strain and struggle out a tiny shit, which she then folded the pad around and returned to her purse. After this, the hostess instructed that we should sit in a circle around the psychic with our eyes closed, arms stretched forward, and fingers spread. Somewhere down the street, little kids were playing tag, and a cat in the side yard was meowing in distress or demand, and there was the smell of jasmine, and of hot dust, and the chihuahua was panting *hha—hha—hha*. It was like a moment from a horror movie—the tactic that is called a jump scare—when the psychic grabbed my wrists. *Your dead*, she said, *are all here.*

Attic

Stop. If you are on the street and look up from this spot, you are looking up at a house on a hill, a house as tall, and narrow, and gray, and toothed with glass as a haunted mansion in a children's stop-motion movie, though this is not a children's stop-motion movie. Though this is not a movie, and though the house is not a mansion, yes, inside it there are bats.

At the bottom of the hill, there is a streetlamp, and you are standing under it, and it turns your skin as yellow as disease as you look up at the house on the hill that could be your home, if you are a runaway returning home again. If you are a runaway, inside the house on the hill there are framed pictures, and you are in them, smiling, and not smiling. If you are a runaway, in the house on the hill that has been your home, there is something, somewhere there that still smells of you. In a closet, or in a cupboard, or cached away and taken out in secret, at night, to be breathed-in and cried-onto by a child you left behind, there is something there in the house on the hill that still smells of you, if you are a runaway from the house, if the house was once your home. If this were a children's stop-motion movie, though this is not a children's stop-motion movie, the crying child would have the soft, purple-vein-patterned wings of a bat. Though this is not a children's stop-motion movie, if this were a children's stop-motion movie, you too would have the soft, purple-vein-patterned wings of a bat, but tied down, close to your body, held tight to your back by a series of cinched-up leather belts, biting into your skin as you stand under the streetlamp, looking up at the house on the hill, but this is not a children's stop-motion movie, and the only bat wings in the house are in the walls, fixed to the furred bodies of bats.

At the bottom of the hill, there is a streetlamp, and the streetlamp has a mildewed glass globe, the light passing through as patchy as a stray, as patchy as the full moon filled with the dark distortion of a boy's pocked face, as patchy as the memory of the nightmare when you wake from it—

You might have thought at first that you were dreaming. You might have been on an adventure with the wild roan horse you had captured and tamed. Together you and the horse have braved sandstorms and blizzards, weaved through spans of rattling, venomous snakes, out run red-eyed wolves. At night, you slap the horse's neck in easy companionship. At sunrise, the horse nuzzles you awake. What is between you and the horse, is the love of a boy and his horse. And then you have to shoot the horse and eat the horse, and you've forgotten its name, but you know it had a name, because you gave it its name, and now you are carrying two five-gallon buckets of guts through a field of blood, and your arms are so tired and your heart is so badly beaten that eventually it will die.

I have to tell you something now. I am sorry, but you are not real. The house on the hill is real. Children's stop-motion movies are real. The bats in the walls are real. The streetlamp is real. The mildew on its glass globe, corrupting the light, is real. Behind the highest window in the house on the hill, there are two girls, and they are real, but you are real only in their nightmare.

Earlier, the girls sat under the high window, sat in the mottled light from the streetlamp, sat getting their little plastic imitation-woman-dolls drunk on water served in pen caps cut to look like tiny blue cups, before slamming them plastic tit to plastic tit, tiny forked dolls' hands catching one another's flammable dolls' hair, acting out the future fights of real women. In this play, there were pauses, one girl passing her little plastic imitation-woman doll to the other, then going to the window, checking the space the streetlamp colors yellow, checking for a boy looking up as she looks down.

If there is any comfort in this, I can tell you that the cat twining its skin and bones body around your grubby shins, rubbing its whiskered cheek against your stained boot, is not real either. It exists only in the texture of the girls' nightmare, which they share between them like they share all things: the bed they sleep in and the blanket pulled over their heads, believing, perhaps, that when you come to murder them, to dash their grandmother's girl-sized, china-headed doll against the dresser and slit their pink throats with a shard of its painted cheek, that the blanket will protect them. They sleep in the attic, and this is where you come from: the attic of memory, full of racoons.

In Texas There Are Tours of Things That Aren't There Anymore

Ten years from now I will think of Texas as the end of girlhood. Hot nights on the thin ledge of the edge of sleep, listening past the quiet to the cockroaches scaling the slick insides of a plastic bag of dinner's discarded odds and ends—the last sweetness in the tiny sauce cup, the salted peel of a potato pursed like a mouth, the final, taffy-yellow bite of brisket-fat spat into a paper napkin, and then the train whistle, punching through, and I am upright, a hard-beating heart, and on the bedside table the cheap plastic fan at the furthest point of its rotation sticks, clicks, and clicks and clicks unable to reverse its course. A shift of the curtains, a spill of dishwater light: good morning.

One hundred years ago, on the spring-fed river boiling cold from the rocks, a silent film star sent to the country to be cured of an unnamed affliction fled the vast verandaed hospital—a gray carcass now on a hill watercolored by wild flowers—and didn't drown, though he dove down and down again, trying in a psychosis of withdrawal to swim through the split where the water roared up.

In the closer past, on the same river, but further down, after the slow flowing tannic stretch, dark as over-steeped tea, where the snouted softshell turtles rise through the red like a quiet corps of color-muted military hot air balloons, I didn't drown.

Caught in a current surge, I submerged, scuffing over river rock, skin stripped back—my chin, my shins, my shoulders, my knuckles, my knees, all singing in a carrying high-note of hurt. When I was beyond breathless, black bursts of tar-bubble-light and raw fingertips reaching nothing, the river calmed again, widening, dropping down into shallow yellow acres of puddle-water. All the young mothers, the straps of their bathing suits pushed from their shoulders so as not to interrupt their tans, laid out on the smooth rock rim, their babies splashing naked.

Once, on the river, there was a concrete coliseum with a cold, spring-fed pool at its center: The Aquarena, where busty girls with pin curls set with Gum of Benjamin who could hold their breath for long minutes showed their athletic ability by performing synchronized tricks with a twitch-snouted series of pink piglets all called Ralphie. *Visit The Aquarena! Home of Ralphie, The World Famous Swimming Pig!*

This began as a love poem and still is.

Literary scholars of certain training and temperament will argue importance indicated by absence. That which never appears, still, they would say, overlaps every shadow and tickles each fine, premonitory hair at the back of every neck.

There are the ready phrases for the pain that accompanies love: swallowed stones, lodged fish bones, homesickness, sitting home alone.

Acknowledgements

Work collected here has appeared, sometimes in an alternate version, in the following journals:

Conduit
Constellations
Ethel Zine
Golden Walkman
Grist
La Vague
Ploughshares
Poet Lore
Poetry Northwest
Slice
Sporklet
The Moth
The Shore
Westerly

JENNY IRISH is from Maine and lives in Arizona, where she teaches in the Creative Writing Program at Arizona State University. She is the author of the collections *Common Ancestor*, *I Am Faithful*, and the forthcoming chapbook *Hatch*.

www.ingramcontent.com/pod-product-compliance
Lightning Source LLC
Chambersburg PA
CBHW082040080526
44578CB00009B/773